Using Realistic Mathematics Education in UK classrooms

Paul Dickinson and Sue Hough

They stopped asking 'What is the point of this?'
They stopped saying 'Can we do something different?'
I stopped replying 'We have to do it because you have an exam/test on it'

It has reinforced for me that learning is a long-term process and that expecting small chunks to be learnt every 15 minutes or so is highly unrealistic.

This booklet is designed to give teachers and students who have used

Realistic Mathematics Education

an opportunity to say how it has made a difference to them.

ISBN: 978-0-948186-24-0

Copy editor: Penny Nicholson

Printed by Heron Press Ltd (01373) 825602

Contents

Introduction

Over the past eight years, the Centre for Mathematics Education at Manchester Metropolitan University (MMU) has been trialling Realistic Mathematics Education (RME), a way of teaching mathematics which is used in the Netherlands. In that time, over 40 schools and 2000 students have been involved in projects at Key Stage 3 and Key Stage 4.

The views of teachers and students have been crucial to the development of the work. With this in mind, a survey of those who have been involved was conducted. This booklet details the responses to that survey and the projects that the teachers have been involved in. There is also a short section of students' work and details of where more of this can be seen. An outline account of Realistic Mathematics Education is also included.

The work at MMU has recently been independently evaluated by the Centre for Education and Monitoring (CEM) at Durham University. The executive summary from this evaluation is at the end of this booklet. The full report can be found at www.mei.org.uk/files/pdf/RME_Evaluation_final_report.pdf.

These trials have resulted in the publication of a series of books based on Realistic Mathematics Education and covering Levels 3–7 of the UK National Curriculum.[1]

For further information about the project, email S.Hough@mmu.ac.uk or P.Dickinson@mmu.ac.uk or stella.dudzic@mei.org.uk.

What is Realistic Mathematics Education?

Philosophy

The philosophy underpinning Realistic Mathematics Education (RME) is that students should develop their mathematical understanding by working from contexts that make sense to them. Initially, they devise their own intuitive methods for working on problems but, using a carefully chosen sequence of examples and appropriate teacher interventions, they then generalise and develop a more formal understanding. This is supported by well-designed textbooks.

An important stage in RME is when students move from their own intuitive mathematical strategies to more sophisticated and formal ways of working. Dutch mathematics educators have developed a variety of ways to secure this transition by using 'models' as a scaffolding device. A thorough analysis of the use of such models has been provided by van den Heuvel-Panhuizen.[2] Because their students' understanding is rooted in contexts and mental images, it is secure.

Comparing classroom approaches

The RME approach is significantly different from the approaches often used in England in a number of respects.

- Use of realistic situations as a means of allowing students to develop their mathematics as opposed to using contexts as applications of the formal mathematics and, occasionally, as scene-setters to introduce a new topic before moving rapidly on to the theory.

- Less emphasis on algorithms and more on making sense and gradual refinement of informal procedures.

- Emphasis on refining and systemising understanding.

- Less emphasis on linking single lessons to direct content acquisition and more on gradual development over a longer period of time. Students stay with a topic for long periods of time, remaining in context throughout.

- Discussion and reflection play a significant part in supporting student development.

- Greater emphasis on research into learning and teaching, and on trialling and refining materials used in schools.

Shown here are some of the displays of goods that can be seen at a local market. In each case, write down how many items you think there are in the display. Also write down whether you think each answer is exact or an estimate.

An example of RME-based materials relating to volume

The name 'Realistic Mathematics Education'

The language, and particularly the words 'context' and 'realistic', used to describe RME can give rise to misunderstanding. The contexts are not necessarily situations where the mathematics is applied to real-world problems; what is important is that they allow students to take ownership of the mathematics. Puzzles, fictitious situations and even formal mathematics can all provide suitable contexts, as long as they are real in the students' minds.

The possibility of misinterpretation is explained by Marja van den Heuvel-Panhuizen from the Freudenthal Institute[3]:

> It must be admitted, the name 'Realistic Mathematics Education' is somewhat confusing ... The reason, however, why the Dutch reform of mathematics education was called 'realistic' is not just the connection with the real world, but is related to the emphasis that RME puts on offering the students problem situations which they can imagine. The Dutch translation of the verb 'to imagine' is 'zich REALISEren'.

A short history of Realistic Mathematics Education

Realistic Mathematics Education in the Netherlands

The Freudenthal Institute (FI), University of Utrecht, was set up in 1971 in response to a perceived need to improve the quality of mathematics teaching in Dutch schools. This led to the development of a research strategy and to a theory of mathematics pedagogy called Realistic Mathematics Education (RME) which is now used throughout Holland. In international mathematics tests, the Netherlands is now considered to be one of the highest achieving countries in the world.[4]

In the Netherlands, RME is intensively researched, trialled and re-evaluated.

RME in the USA – *Mathematics in Context*

In 1991, the University of Wisconsin, funded by National Science Foundation (USA), in collaboration with the Freudenthal Institute started to develop the *Mathematics in Context* approach based on RME. The initial materials were drafted by staff from the Freudenthal Institute on the basis of 20 years of experience of curriculum development. After revision by staff from the University of Wisconsin, the material was trialled, revised and retrialled over a period of five years. The trialling not only involved checking a variety of versions of questions for effectiveness but also the careful examination of student strategies and of teacher needs, beliefs and expectations.

The first version of *Mathematics in Context* was published in 1996 and it has undergone several revisions since then. The teacher material, which supports the student books, provides a comprehensive analysis of issues pertaining to each topic and provides the teacher with insights into teaching and learning trajectories. There is also a comprehensive support infrastructure for teachers using *Mathematics in Context*.

Mathematics in Context has been adopted by a considerable number of school districts and has produced impressive student achievement; this is described in the 2003 book *Standards-based School Mathematics Curricula*.[5]

See also Romberg (2001)[6] for a valuable summary of design and research features of *Mathematics in Context*, including the influence on teacher behaviours and beliefs about teaching and on their perception of student capability.

RME in the UK

Key Stage 3

In 2003, The Centre for Mathematics Education at Manchester Metropolitan University (MMU) purchased a set of *Mathematics in Context* materials and trialled them with Year 7 classes in a local school. The reaction to the materials was extremely positive with a real sense that this approach was worthy of continued exploration.

As a consequence of this, the Gatsby Foundation agreed to fund MMU to run a project based around trialling RME (utilising *Mathematics in Context*) with Key Stage 3 students; over twenty schools were involved over a three-year period.

The Economic and Social Research Council (ESRC) also agreed to fund an examination of how teachers' beliefs and behaviours change as a result of engagement in the project. (See Hanley *et al* (2007)[7] for an account of the research into the changes in teachers involved in the project.)

The project focused on three main issues.

▪ Developing an understanding of RME in an English context

▪ Understanding how students develop

▪ Supporting teachers to develop practical skills and a deep knowledge of RME

In terms of student development, over three years the project team saw evidence that students' approaches to solving problems changed and that this influenced how they understood the mathematics. Some details of this are given in the 'Students' work' section on page 17; other findings of the project were described by Dickinson and Eade (2005).[8]

Key Stage 4

As the original project ended, teacher enthusiasm for continuing with this approach at Key Stage 4 led to the launch of a new project, *Making Sense of Maths*. This began in 2007 with Foundation tier students and is now being extended to include both tiers of the two-tier GCSE. The project runs in collaboration with the Freudenthal Institute (FI) in the Netherlands and with Mathematics in Education and Industry (MEI) in the UK and is partially funded by the Esmée Fairbairn Foundation.

The Foundation tier resources consist of ten booklets, written by MMU and FI staff, covering the Key Stage 4 Foundation tier curriculum. These booklets build upon the experiences gained from the Key Stage 3 project and take account of difficulties highlighted by the Key Stage 3 teachers, such as the need for RME-based materials which feature British contexts and are a better preparation for the questions in UK national tests.

The project has involved Foundation tier classes from six schools in the first cohort and ten schools in the second cohort. MMU has supplied resources to these schools and has provided ongoing support in the form of twilight training sessions and school-based observations. Feedback given by the teachers has been used to revise the materials.

As a result of the very positive feedback from teachers, as exemplified in this booklet, materials are now being produced for Higher tier GCSE, with trials following a similar pattern.

Evidence for the effectiveness of RME

Teachers using RME report that it enables more students to understand mathematics and to engage with it. However, it is not easy to measure the effectiveness of a way of teaching, particularly when its aims are not quite the same as those in conventional classrooms. (RME places more emphasis on understanding and problem solving).

The performance of the Netherlands in international comparisons of mathematical attainment has been consistently strong over recent years. The two major international comparative studies are the Programme for International Student Assessment (PISA) and the Trends in International Mathematics and Science Study (TIMSS). The former compares students' mathematical problem-solving abilities and is administered by the Organisation for Economic Co-operation and Development (OECD), the latter measures purely mathematical attainment. The Netherlands usually scores well above average in both tests.

A 2005 study[9] into the instructional effectiveness of *Mathematics in Context* in the United States concluded as follows.

- Following the adoption of *Mathematics in Context*, across these schools in these four states, the percentage of students scoring at the lowest levels of achievement on state-wide mathematics tests declined significantly.

- Following the adoption of *Mathematics in Context*, across these schools in these four states, the percentage of students scoring at the proficient and higher levels of achievement on state-wide mathematics tests increased significantly.

Quantitative and attitudinal data were collected from all schools involved in the two UK projects: Key Stage 3, using *Mathematics in Context* and Key Stage 4, using *Making Sense of Maths*. Project classes were matched with control groups. Similar data were also collected from matched schools that had had no contact with the project; this was necessary because teaching methods had been shared between some teachers in project schools, allowing the spread of RME to non-project classes.

The data have been presented at a number of conferences and feature in their proceedings. These include the International Group for the Psychology of Mathematics Education (2006) and the British Society for Research into Learning Mathematics (2005, 2010, 2011). Generally speaking, students from the RME project classes were more likely to get correct answers to questions and also more likely to approach questions in a way which showed they understood them.

In 2011, Mathematics in Education and Industry (MEI) commissioned an evaluation by the Centre for Education and Monitoring (CEM) at Durham University.[10] As part of this evaluation, teachers involved in the projects were interviewed. The evaluation reported:

> These teachers generally agree that pupils are much more positive about mathematics compared to those taught by more traditional methods.

This evaluation also reanalysed some assessment data using Rasch modelling, comparing the achievement and understanding of a group of students who had experienced RME with a matched group who had not. The evaluation found that:

> The results indicated those pupils who had experienced RME were not only more likely to solve a problem correctly, but showed considerably more understanding through their ability to explain their strategy.

The teachers on the MiC project were also the subject of a research study funded by ESRC and carried out by a research team from MMU.[11]

Numerous other articles have been written by members of the project team. A list can be found at the end of this booklet, together with other useful articles and resources. In addition to these, the Freudenthal Institute Wiki gives an overview of RME and links to research articles.[12]

Comments from teachers

Teachers were asked for their views under a number of headings. Some of these are reproduced here, together with a summary of the teachers' overall experience.

Impact on classroom practice

RME represented a very different way of working in the classroom and hence presented a significant challenge to the teachers concerned. Initially, change would only be seen when working with the materials and with project classes, but slowly teachers began to report significant change in how they approached teaching in all of their classes. In this respect, the projects had a real impact on the professional practice of those involved, with the teachers undergoing significant shifts in their understanding and beliefs about the teaching and learning of mathematics. The quotes below expand on this.

> Recently an OFSTED inspector watched my lesson and commented on the fact that pupils felt safe and not afraid to make mistakes. He also commented on how the mistakes were used as teaching points and that pupils were helping each other to work through these misconceptions. This atmosphere had been developed by using *Maths In Context* techniques. Pupils feel more confident in 'having a go' because there is always a way in for them to access a problem.
> The lesson was graded as 'outstanding'!
>
> *Assistant Head, previously Head of Mathematics*

> Since becoming aware of the RME approach to teaching maths I am certain that the use of models and contexts has influenced every aspect of my teaching. I am convinced that students engage more readily with the content and can make their own sense of the mathematics, and evidence, in terms of results and reduced behavioural issues due to engagement, backs this up.
>
> *Project teacher, recently promoted to Head of Mathematics*

> The first group I tried MSM materials on was a Year 10, set 5 out of 8, which contained a number of disaffected pupils. There was an outspoken and often difficult pupil who disliked maths intensely after a long history of 'failing' at it. After about a term of working with the MSM materials, at the end of one lesson she told me that it was the first time she had got to the end of a maths lesson without wanting to cry. After spending nine years struggling to comprehend the way maths is conventionally taught in this country, the approach of MSM materials was so different that it significantly improved the motivation and engagement levels of these pupils. Instead of meeting the same old topics in the same old ways, they were able to get stuck into real problems, often without realising what the 'traditional', old (and previously hated!) content was until they were halfway through and already succeeding.
> The dreaded chants of 'but when are we ever going to use this, Miss' just melt away when using MSM materials.
>
> *Project teacher, now an Advanced Skills Teacher*

The MiC/MSM resources have had an enormous impact on how I teach mathematics. In fact, the entire philosophy behind their approach to learning has influenced the way I prepare all of my lessons. I now think I better understand how children really learn maths and what I need to do to support them.

Project teacher, now an Advanced Skills Teacher

These materials enabled pupils to discuss their ideas with insight and with confidence. The pupils are encouraged to use their own methods and so, with time, are able to explain these to others and to defend them. The starting contexts are rich and sometimes low ability pupils do not realise they are doing maths; this can only be a good thing for pupils who have so little confidence in the subject.

The materials also give a teacher great insight into how pupils think and this became by far the most powerful way of 'assessment for learning'. Several pupils achieved significantly higher than their predictors using this approach.

I even heard some Foundation pupils discussing maths problems outside the classroom door! And when it comes to revision, these pupils are much better able to recall a helpful context, such as cheese cubes for volume or subway sandwiches for fractions, than they ever were some meaningless mathematical procedure.

I could not have made these materials myself but now, whatever age of pupil I am teaching, I cannot help but approach the mathematics in this way.

Co-ordinator for Mathematics in a Mathematics specialist school

Working with the MiC/MSM material and the associated training/professional development has changed my entire approach to teaching because it has changed my entire view of how children learn maths. I now appreciate the need to find this 'common ground' and establish a common starting point – that everyone has been able to access – before embarking on the maths. The use of discussion is essential if students are going to refine their understanding of mathematical concepts and how they relate to each other.

Project teacher, now Head of Mathematics

The models introduced to me through RME are now integral to my teaching of mathematics.

The ratio table and RME's use of the number line quickly moved to all my teaching, across the age and ability range.

I now very rarely teach without a context, and rarely evaluate a non-context based lesson as effective. RME has altered my understanding of the way in which people learn and work with mathematics.

Head of Mathematics

I have never taught fractions the same way again since using MiC materials. The contexts in which the pupils need to work not only engage them but push them to think and justify their ideas. I like the way that it stays with the informal setting for a long time whereas, historically, you would find an equivalent fraction, etc. It now actually makes sense to some pupils rather than a set of rules. Why did I ever try to use algorithms with Level 3 pupils? They learnt much more using informal methods.

Project teacher

When explaining something, my first instinct is now to draw something. I have also now recognised how visual I am myself as a learner (and how much I struggle with purely aural information).

Models frequently occur in mechanics. I now recognise that the models/diagrams that I always assumed made sense to students may be too abstract/formal for them to engage with.

I now feel comfortable/confident in developing a context to engage the class in the lesson and in the maths. I think I always thought maths should be kept realistic and now I always look for a physical example to allow access to the maths. Sometimes this might involve a model, sometimes it might involve a 'people activity' or a scaled down demonstration.

Head of Mathematics

The need for 'purpose' in the maths classroom is a major issue for me. There must be a reason for answering a question or solving a problem otherwise, why bother? Maths must be seen to be the useful subject that it is.

Project teacher explaining how MiC gave this 'sense of purpose'

One principle of RME is that the pupils are making progress when they are articulating their thoughts and when they can explain their actions. They are making little jumps in understanding by thinking about what they need to do and how they will attempt it, and explaining it to others. I like to observe this in class, whether they are a project group or not. I always like to have time to talk about what we need to do and how we are going to try and do it, even if the lesson is not very investigative or explorative.

I also like to have time later in the lesson to talk about what we have done. I also think it is important to answer their questions, if they are trying to process a concept they need to be able to question different aspects of it. I think all of this comes from my reading, practising and understanding of RME.

Project teacher

It's my first year of teaching and I love it ... and the pupils know what they are talking about and can explain ... that is how I look at their progression.

Newly qualified teacher, project teacher

Continuing Professional Development

In addition to support meetings directly linked to the projects, a number of other professional development courses have arisen from the projects. These include a Master's module on teaching using RME (run by one of the original project teachers), a series of one-day courses run at MMU, and numerous workshops and presentations at conferences such as those run by the Association of Teachers of Mathematics, Mathematics in Education and Industry, the National Association for Numeracy and Mathematics in Colleges, the British Educational Research Association, the British Congress of Mathematics Education, the British Society for Research into Learning Mathematics and the International Group for the Psychology of Mathematics Education.

Many of the original project teachers have themselves become advocates for RME and have run workshops and training sessions at many CPD events and teacher conferences. In addition, at the time of writing, three teachers from the projects are writing Master's dissertations based on their work in the classroom.

Some typical comments from the project teachers relating to professional development are given below.

> My experiences have given me the starting point, and then the substance, to allow me to complete two-thirds of a Master's degree.

> Interaction with staff from other schools [on the project] has created rich opportunities for sharing good practice.

> I was mainly involved for my own interest and as a research project for my Master's, but [the project] has definitely enhanced my professional development. The research, readings, and discussions about education help me to continue improving my practice and maintaining an interest in doing so.

> My involvement with the project gave me the confidence to run CPD sessions for other teachers in my school. I have now done many of these, and also some for teachers from other schools in my area.

> The project sparked off lots of opportunities for me to present my experiences at school, local, and national level. I have presented a workshop at a national CPD event, and a showcase session at the National Specialist Colleges Conference.

Impact on schools and further dissemination

While teachers were describing how the projects were influencing their own classrooms, it became apparent that other teachers in the school were also beginning to be influenced. The sharing of ideas at departmental meetings, School INSET and Local Authority training events were all affecting this. Indeed, it became almost impossible to use data from 'control' (i.e. non-project) groups within a project school, such was the level of infiltration of MiC ideas. The comments below serve to exemplify this unintended outcome.

Since involvement with the projects began we have had four new members of staff – all having MiC experience as part of their ITT programme. All of these staff have a comfortable approach to using context. I would say they naturally incorporate context into the majority of their lesson planning – certainly, they feel that there is 'something missing' if they plan a predominantly abstract lesson. The department don't all use the MiC/MSM material with all of their classes; however, they all dip in and out of it when appropriate. Also, MiC/MSM material always plays a big part in departmental Learning and Teaching Inset. Discussion (and good questioning) is an important part of all department lessons and our experiences with MiC/MSM have helped develop this.

MiC really made me question the way pupils think. I believe this has made me more confident about the issues around learning and teaching and so helped me with career progression.
Also, being part of the project gave me the opportunity to take risks which has led to improved pupil performance and understanding. This is something that I can use to illustrate how to move departments and individuals forward and embrace change.

My department has been mixed about embracing MiC. I believe that is because it is delivered in a completely different way to traditional lessons. The fact that you can't just pick up a book and pick an exercise would really knock the confidence of some.
Luckily, there are quite a few members of the department who use the material regularly and share findings. It has even been a factor that has attracted applications to vacant posts within the department and been the focus of observation requests from other schools.
I have also begun to roll out a Year 6 MiC transition unit to our feeder primaries, taking the work beyond our department.
One member of the department is currently working with Primary colleagues and supporting them in the delivery of one of the books.

Impact on teacher beliefs

Working with RME represents a significant shift in how many teachers view the learning and teaching of mathematics. It was recognised at the outset of the projects that teachers would experience some discomfort as previously held (and often long-standing) beliefs were challenged. Indeed, one of the aims of the original project was to examine how teachers' beliefs did change over time. This was also the subject of an ESRC research project.[13]

> RME has influenced my understanding of maths learning since my training, and consequently has not so much altered my thinking as developed it. The apparent simplicity of the models and use of contexts hides a fundamental shift in how students approach the learning of mathematics, when compared to the way in which I studied maths at school. Often there has been discussion concerning the importance of a commitment to the use of RME that goes beyond ordinary CPD – almost a cult like following, with some staff appearing to reject it due to apathy or even mistrust. This seems to stem from the magnitude of the shift in thinking that can occur.

> Working with the projects has significantly changed my beliefs. I believe that learning maths is a process of fitting together new information/experiences with what pupils already 'understand' (or believe they understand) about the world. Maths is an active subject, not about memory but about problem solving.

> Exposing students to new, rich contexts and at the same time highlighting the 'mathematical' elements of these situations, allows children to learn maths that they see as 'relevant' but that also contains all the 'abstract' content that they would learn in a more 'traditional' classroom setting. I now believe we don't (and it is dangerous if we do) create a false mathematical environment for students to learn from – the maths is all 'out there', it just needs presenting to the pupils carefully and thoughtfully.

> Working on the project has definitely changed my beliefs about teaching. I no longer push to the abstract too quickly and keep thinking about what models can be used again and again to cement understanding of skills.

> It has reinforced for me that learning is a long-term process and that expecting small chunks to be learnt every 15 minutes or so is highly unrealistic.

> It has made me appreciate that the pupils' sense of what I was teaching may not be the same as my sense of what I was teaching.

Impact on students

Anything which effected such a significant shift in teacher practices and beliefs was inevitably going to impact significantly on students and this impact has been monitored throughout the projects. Data were gathered from students at regular intervals; detailed quantitative analysis of data can be found in the evaluation[14], though at the end of this section we have included a small amount of students' work. Mainly, however, we are concerned here with the comments from students and teachers.

Teachers' comments

The project has had a huge influence on my classes. The students show much more confidence when working with maths 'in context'. There is much less of a correct/incorrect environment created in lessons (compared to a more traditional approach) and so the students are not frightened to 'have a go' as much.

The students may not necessarily say that they like working with the material, however. This is (I feel) because the demands the work makes on students – in terms of thinking skills and reasoning – are much higher than a more traditional approach. Students are required to 'think' for almost a full lesson when taught in this way. Compare this with a more traditional approach when students spend a large proportion of lessons 'practising' a mathematical skill in some way.

I've not had any kids yet this year say, 'Why are we doing this,' and that's unusual.

Many of my students now 'see' connections between different areas of maths themselves, without having to be prompted. They point out connections between the maths we do in lessons and 'things' they do in other lessons, or at home, much more freely and naturally.
I feel that my students naturally think much more logically and 'mathematically' when taught using contexts. When students learn maths through contexts they are directly engaging with the maths themselves. They are learning maths by directly solving problems with the maths rather than learning it 'second-hand' through my explanation of the maths.

One of my best pupils (A* in Year 10) said that MiC had given him so many strategies for figuring out Higher Maths that he didn't need to keep running for help. Ratio tables have made a lot of work easier for most pupils. Arrow strings have stopped a lot losing marks at GCSE. It just makes pupils more prepared to have a go – great for functional type questions.

I think the fact that they will have a go or think of a 'way in' does signify a difference in attitude as, previously, they would just sit and wait to be spoon fed.

They stopped asking 'What is the point of this?'
They stopped saying 'Can we do something different?'
I stopped replying 'We have to do it because you have an exam/test on it'
Energy levels were higher in the lessons. A lot more discussion took place. There was more interest/enthusiasm in the classroom.

The importance the resources place on discussion and sharing ideas has changed the atmosphere in our classroom. My students are so much more confident and prepared to have-a-go at maths that is unfamiliar.

I now never hear students ask 'when are we ever going to use this?'. Their enthusiasm for the subject, as well as the belief that they can do well, has grown dramatically.

The use of context builds pupils' confidence to engage with a variety of problems in an intuitive way. Pupils are encouraged to work as informally as they need to in order to really understand and be able to justify what they are doing. By delaying the need to rush into formal mathematics, pupils can build this secure understanding, which they can (and often do) fall back on as the problems become more difficult.

Solving 'real' problems improved pupils' motivation to engage with the maths. The contexts used are genuinely interesting and pupils are able to bring their own outside experiences to contribute to lessons, which helps to bring the subject matter to life.

If I was going to make an analogy: we, say, teach them to make a chair and then to make a table whereas what this scheme is doing is helping to create a set of tools that you can use for different things.

Students' comments

They are different because they have one section/book for each subject so you don't have one subject and then go straight onto another. They help you by giving good information; it's also fun because there is a little story to go with each few questions.

I would say they were good because they have some interesting, brain-teasing problems which make you work your socks off, and some easy ones. I would definitely recommend.

I found it much more involving this year (e.g. getting up to the board) and I have felt I've learnt a lot more on fractions.

It has got harder but we concentrate more about the method, rather than the question, so I have definitely improved.

Funner, and different and makes you think about things differently.

Shows different methods of doing maths.

It's easier to understand with all the pictures they use.

Fun and a bit easier.

Had useful methods
Easier to understand.

The work can be difficult but easy at times.

It helps me understand maths that I wouldn't understand in normal text books.

Helps me understand algebra in ways that will help me in the future. E.g. how to add large amounts using value N.

It's helped me understand certain questions and how to work them out.

I think it has helped me understand things a bit better but could be a bit long and boring at times.
[Well, you can't win them all!]

Students' work

The main data analysed quantitatively came from problem solving tests given to both project and control classes from project schools. More detailed accounts of these data can be found in articles referenced at the end of this booklet.

As well as some significant gains in terms of correct answers, a notable feature of the project students' work was the methods and strategies that they used to solve problems. No longer were they content to just manipulate numbers (which was very common in the 'control' classes); they employed strategies which clearly made sense to them. This was most striking with lower attaining students, even when final answers were incorrect.

Here we focus on just one of the questions, which involved finding the area of a trapezium. This was considered to be problem solving as the Year 7 students attempting the question had not yet met the formula for the area of this shape.

The question was

Find the area of the shape shown below.

Show carefully how you worked it out.

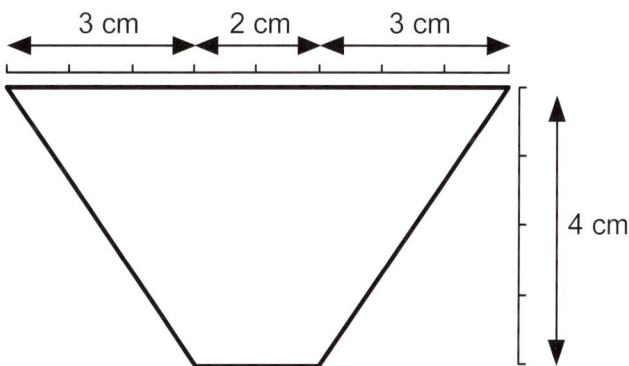

The vast majority of control students adopted a purely numerical method, often simply adding, multiplying or in some way averaging the numbers on display. The following example of a control student's work shows this.

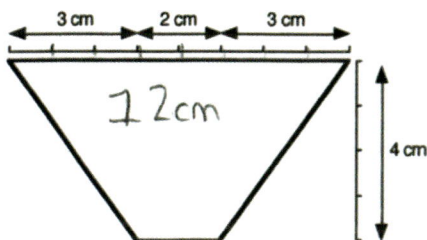

I got this becouse 3×2×3×4 = 48 and the I divided by 4 becaue there a 4 numbers.

Less than a third of control students adopted a strategy which 'made sense' or could in any way lead to a correct answer. With project students, however, over three-quarters of them attempted a 'sensible' strategy, ranging from drawing centimetre squares and counting, through splitting into a rectangle and triangles, to moving a triangle to create a rectangle. Although these did not always lead to a correct answer, it was encouraging to see how many students had developed a sense of what area is really about. For example, the following project student does not get a correct answer but clearly has an understanding of what area is.

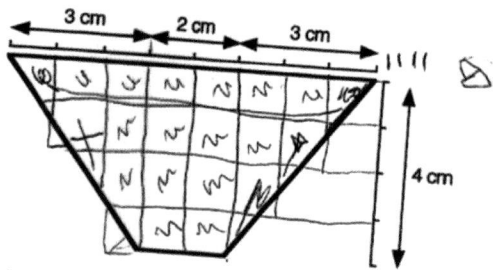

Show carefully how you worked it out.

3 cm   2 cm   3 cm

4 cm

15 whole squares.

I divided the shape into squares and counted how many whole squares there was there was 15. I then added pieces to other piece to make them whole and I got 4½ I added this to 15 so it was the area of 19 ½

The following project student successfully uses a reallocating strategy to find the area.

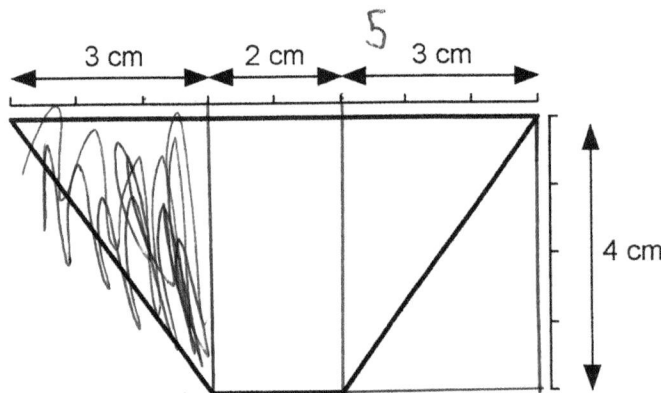

3 cm   2 cm   5   3 cm

4 cm

5 cm × 4 cm = 20 cm²

By contrast, the approach of most control students can be summed up in the response of one of them who commented:

> I can't remember how to work out this area, but I do know that it is something to do with timesing!

This approach is exemplified in the work of the control student below who tries two different multiplication approaches, with no attempt to make sense of the problem from an area perspective.

Executive summary from the independent evaluation

For the full evaluation go to www.mei.org.uk/files/pdf/RME_Evaluation_final_report.pdf.

Realistic Mathematics Education (RME) is realistic in that children learn mathematics through engaging in solving problems in contexts that are meaningful to them. RME originated from the Freudenthal Institute in the Netherlands in the 1970s to meet a perceived need to improve the quality of mathematics teaching in Dutch schools. Following the success of RME in Holland this approach to teaching and learning mathematics was taken up in the 1990s in Wisconsin in the USA within a project called *Mathematics in Context* (MiC). In 2003 researchers from Manchester Metropolitan University (MMU) purchased a set of MiC materials, with a view to training teachers to use them in a project based in some of the local schools. It was considered essential for the success of the project that teachers had an understanding of the philosophy of the RME approach and its underpinning theory of how children learn mathematics.

MMU obtained funding from the Gatsby Foundation to pilot the RME project using MiC materials. This pilot project ran from 2004 to 2006. It was aimed principally at lower ability KS3 pupils, particularly those in Year 7. In 2007 MMU began work on developing the RME approach for KS4 pupils; the project was called Making Sense of Mathematics (MSM), and was, again, targeted at lower ability pupils, aiming for Foundation tier GCSE. It was hoped that this project would help these pupils have a positive and meaningful experience of mathematics as well as helping them to achieve at GCSE. MSM materials are currently being developed for use with more able pupils aiming for the Higher tier GCSE.

The Gatsby funded project was evaluated at the time, but there has been no subsequent evaluation of the development of RME and the MiC and MSM projects. The curriculum development body, Mathematics in Education and Industry (MEI) became interested in the RME approach, believing this approach has the potential to make a substantial contribution to mathematics education and is supporting the projects at MMU. MEI has commissioned this evaluation.

The evaluation comprises both qualitative and quantitative methods.

Qualitative methods

Interviews, by telephone and face-to-face, were conducted with teachers currently using MiC and/or trialling the MSM materials to discern their experiences, views and any issues involved in using the RME approach. These interviews were enhanced through observation of some of these teachers using the RME approach in their classrooms with pupils and also by interviewing some of their pupils.

Outcomes: These teachers are enthusiastic, and believe in the philosophy of RME, finding it a natural way for children to learn mathematics. They emphasised that it is essential that teachers understand the philosophy and are trained in the use of the materials, highlighting that 'you can't just pick up the books and use them; it will not be effective'. These teachers believe the RME approach develops a better understanding of mathematics in their pupils than more traditional methods.

Teachers reported that the contexts and related activities interest the pupils and so engage them in the lesson. Their pupils experience a range of activities, including practical work and discussion. Discussion at various levels, in pairs, in a group or whole class is an essential part of the RME approach.

Formal statements of objectives given at the start of the lesson and traditional formal lesson plans can be a hindrance rather than a help in the RME approach, but teachers need to be well prepared, well organised and have appropriate resources for activities to hand. They note it may take several lessons for pupils to internalise the models they work with, but, once they do, they can understand how these models can be applied in a variety of contexts.

Pupils are generally receptive to the RME approach. They enjoy working together to solve the problems and sharing their strategies and solutions with each other. They look forward to mathematics lessons.

The transcripts of interviews with teachers who participated in the Gatsby project were available and analysed, with teachers reporting much the same views about RME as the current interviewees.

Quantitative methods

Some assessment data from Year 7 pupils from the 2004–06 MiC project were reanalysed using Rasch modelling. This compared achievement and understanding of pupils who had experienced RME with a matched group of pupils who had not. The results indicated those pupils who had experienced RME were not only more likely to solve a problem correctly, but showed considerably more understanding through their ability to explain their strategy.

Emerging issues

1   Progress and assessment

There is concern, from parents and school management, that pupils write little in their exercise books and so, apparently, do little work in mathematics lessons. There is little formal assessment, as such, with assessment largely based on teacher judgement. There is an issue of what is an appropriate form of assessment for KS3 pupils being taught through RME methods.

2   Preparation for GCSE

There is concern over perceived incompatibility of GCSE questions and RME type problems. Teachers have to compromise their methods in KS4 to enhance their pupils' chances of success at GCSE. This may be alleviated by the new (from 2010) GCSEs, including the Applications of Mathematics GCSE, and also the functional skills requirement. Teachers believe pupils taught using the RME approach will be well prepared for these new assessments, but no evidence, as such, is available yet.

3   Pupils experiencing a mix of approaches

In many schools RME has not been adopted by the whole of the mathematics teaching staff. Some prefer more traditional methods, based on a three part structured lesson plan and an explicit lesson objective, and see no reason to change. Pupils are likely to experience both types of teacher as they progress through the year groups. This may confuse pupils; is it a problem? Teachers are generally agreed that imposing RME on unwilling colleagues will not be successful.

4 Development of the use of RME

For committed teachers who believe in the approach, RME is very successful. However, to develop effectively and to involve more teachers, a support network that can offer initial training and ongoing professional development is essential. The MMU model, with the university project team at the heart of a network of teachers participating in the project, would seem an ideal model.

The success of the project for these teachers and the leadership from MMU needs a mechanism for dissemination to encourage take up and development in other cities. A publication that focuses on the experiences of teachers and pupils who have used RME with positive outcomes, is the recommended way forward, together with presentations at conferences and similar events by the MMU team.

Moving forward

The evaluation has highlighted four 'emerging issues'. Initial thoughts on how to take action on them are given below.

1 Progress and assessment

Parents and school senior managers need information to help them understand the RME approach. Some schools have meetings with parents to explain RME; this has been found to work well. Another possible approach is to produce an explanatory booklet.

It is common in other countries for teacher judgements to be used to assess student progress; however, appropriate ways of recording and communicating such judgements need to be found.

2 Preparation for GCSE

It is hoped that changes to GCSE Mathematics, including the increased emphasis on problem solving and the move to end-of-course assessment, will encourage a stronger emphasis on teaching for understanding. This will help many teachers, including those adopting an RME approach.

3 Students experiencing a mix of approaches

Not enough is known about the effect of a mix of approaches on students. There is scope for further research here. However, it is hoped that the use of RME will become more widespread and that, as a result, more teachers will feel confident to embrace this different way of working.

4 Development of the use of RME

This booklet has been published to help disseminate information about the RME approach to teaching and learning mathematics, taking up the suggestion in the external evaluation. Further consideration will be given to forming appropriate support networks for interested teachers.

References

1   www.hoddereducation.co.uk/Schools/Mathematics/Making-Sense-of-Maths.aspx

2   Van den Heuvel-Panhuizen, M. (2003) The didactical use of models in realistic mathematics education: an example from a longitudinal trajectory on percentage; *Educational Studies in Mathematics 54, 9–35*

3   Van den Heuvel-Panhuizen, M. (2002) Realistic Mathematics Education as work in progress; available at www.fisme.science.uu.nl/publicaties/literatuur/4966.pdf

4   TIMSS (1999, 2007, 2011), PISA (2000, 2006, 2009)

5   *Standards-based School Mathematics Curricula: What are they? What do students learn?*, (2003) edited by Senk, S.L. and Thompson, D.R., can be previewed on Google Books.

6   Romberg, T.A. (2001) Mathematics in Context, Education Development Center, Inc.

7   Hanley, U., Darby, S., and Torrance, H. (2007) Investigating and developing effective strategies for mathematics teaching at KS3 of the English National Curriculum; ESRC Ref: RES-000-22-1082

8, 11   Dickinson, P. and Eade, F. (2005) Trialling Realistic Mathematics Education (RME) in English secondary schools; *Proceedings of the British Society for Research into Learning Mathematics 25 (3)*

9   Holt, Rinehart And Winston Department Of Research And Curriculum, (2005) A Longitudinal Study of the Instructional Effectiveness of Mathematics in Context; available at www.middletowncityschools.com/administration/departments/math/educators/middle/pdf/mic_research.pdf

10, 13, 14   Searle, J. and Barmby, P., (2012) Evaluation Report on the Realistic Mathematics Evaluation Pilot Project; available at www.mei.org.uk/files/pdf/RME_Evaluation_final_report.pdf

12   www.fi.uu.nl/en/wiki/index.php/Realistic_Mathematics_Education

Further reading

Related directly to the project

Dickinson, P. and Eade, F. (2005) Trialling Realistic Mathematics Education (RME) in English secondary schools; *Proceedings of the British Society for Research into Learning Mathematics 25 (3)*

Dickinson, P. and Eade, F. (2006) Exploring Realistic Mathematics Education in English Secondary Schools; *Proceedings of the International Group for the Psychology of Mathematics Education 30 (3)*

Dickinson, P., Eade, F, Gough, S., and Hough, S. (2010) Using Realistic Mathematics Education with low to middle attaining pupils in secondary schools; *Proceedings of the British Society for Research into Learning Mathematics 30 (1)*

Dickinson, P., Hough, S., Searle, J. and Barmby, P. (2011) Evaluating the impact of a Realistic Mathematics Education project in secondary schools; *Proceedings of the British Society for Research into Learning Mathematics 31 (3)*

Hanley, U. and Darby S. (2007) Working with curriculum innovation: teacher identity and the development of viable practice; *Research in Mathematics Education 8*, 53–66

Hanley, U., Darby, S., and Torrance, H. (2007) Investigating and developing effective strategies for mathematics teaching at KS3 of the English National Curriculum; ESRC Ref: RES-000-22-1082

Searle, J. and Barmby, P., (2012) Evaluation Report on the Realistic Mathematics Evaluation Pilot Project; available at www.mei.org.uk/files/pdf/RME_Evaluation_final_report.pdf

www.hoddereducation.co.uk/Schools/Mathematics/Making-Sense-of-Maths.aspx

Related to Realistic Mathematics Education

Anghileri, J., Beishuizen, M. and van Putten, K. (2002) From informal strategies to structured procedures: mind the gap! *Educational Studies in Mathematics 49*, 149–170

Fosnot, C.T. and Dolk, M. (2002) *Young Mathematicians at Work: Constructing Fractions, Decimals, and Percents*; Heinemann

Hodgen, J., Küchemann, D. and Brown, M. (2009) *Secondary students' understanding of mathematics 30 years on*; British Educational Research Association

Romberg, T. A. and Pedro, J. D. (1996) Developing Mathematics in Context: a research process; Madison: National Center for Research in Mathematical Sciences Education

Romberg, T.A. (2001) Mathematics in Context, Education Development Center, Inc.

Treffers, A. (1991) RME in the Netherlands 1980–1990; in Streefland, L. (Ed.) *RME in primary school*; Utrecht: Freudenthal Institute

Treffers, A. and Beishuizen, M. (1999) RME in the Netherlands; in Thompson I. (Ed.) *Issues in teaching numeracy in primary schools*; Buckingham: Open University Press

Van den Heuvel-Panhuizen, M. (2003) The didactical use of models in realistic mathematics education: an example from a longitudinal trajectory on percentage; *Educational Studies in Mathematics 54*, 9–35

Abbreviations used in this document

CPD   Continuing Professional Development

ESRC   The Economic and Social Research Council

FI   Freudenthal Institute

GCSE   General Certificate of Secondary Education

INSET   In Service Training

ITT   Initial teacher training

MiC   Mathematics in Context

MEI   Mathematics in Education and Industry

MMU   Manchester Metropolitan University

MSM   Making Sense of Mathematics

OFSTED   The Office for Standards in Education

PISA   Programme for International Student Assessment

RME   Realistic Mathematics Education

TIMSS   Trends in International Mathematics and Science Study